The Murphy Collective LLC

Original Books, Art, & Crafts

www.themurphycollective.com

Scan to Shop

The Murphy Collective LLC

Grand Memories

by Dustin Murphy

Illustrated by Molly J. Frantz

Published by Orange Hat Publishing 2021
ISBN 9781645382775

www.orangehatpublishing.com

In loving memory of Robert R. Hafner and Robert T. Murphy. Thank you for all the wonderful memories.

Favorite memories with Grandpa include many things,

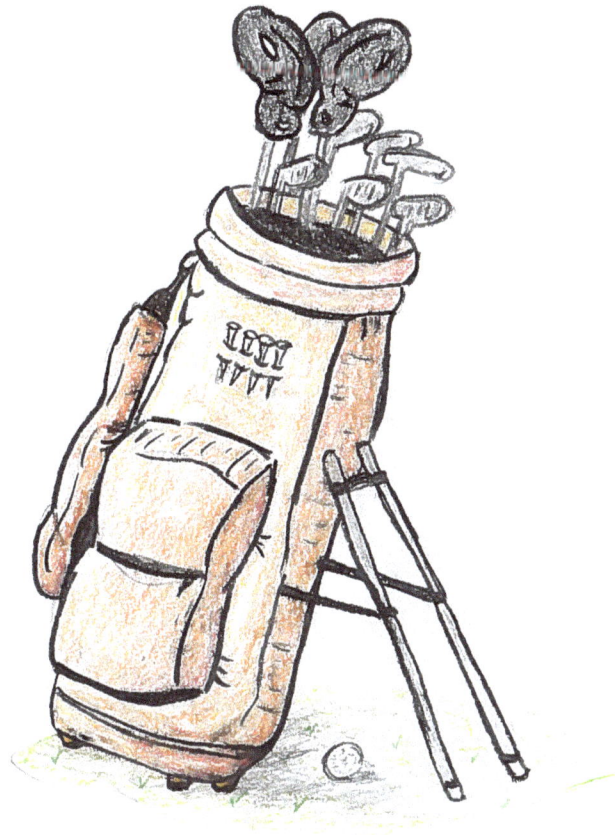

Boat rides and golf clubs,

and feathery wings,

Guitars, harmonicas, and singing a chord,

Fishing all day from boats and from shore.

Holidays and hunting, big smiles and warm hugs

Are just a small part

of the Grandpa we love.

Telling old stories of days out of sight

while playing fun card games with family at night.

Sweet treats, many laughs, and a big flannel coat,

We cherish fondly all of your love and support.

You share your farm stories and love of the land,

And you never withdraw
from giving a hand.

Your heart and your memories have a lasting place

With the family and friends that you embrace.

Dear Grandpa with love,
Wherever is home,
Please know we will take you
Wherever we go.

www.ingramcontent.com/pod-product-compliance
Lightning Source LLC
Chambersburg PA
CBHW040850100426
42813CB00015B/2765

* 9 7 8 1 6 4 5 3 8 2 7 7 5 *